COMPOSER SHOWCASE

HAL LEONARD STUDENT PIANO LIBRARY

Animals Have Feelings Too

EIGHT ORIGINAL PIANO SOLOS

BY JENNIFER LINN

CONTENTS

ISBN 978-1-4950-2791-8

HAL•LEONARD®
CORPORATION

7777 W. BLUEMOUND RD. P.O. BOX 13819 MILWAUKEE, WI 53213

In Australia Contact:
Hal Leonard Australia Pty. Ltd.
4 Lentara Court
Cheltenham, Victoria, 3192 Australia
Email: ausadmin@halleonard.com.au

Visit Hal Leonard Online at
www.halleonard.com

Early Elementary

Bear Determination

Jennifer Linn

Steady and brave (♩ = 132)

Right be - fore hi - ber - na - tion, bears have de -

ter - mi - na - tion: Find some food and fat - ten up.

Win - ter's al - most here! Time for sur - vi - val mode, a

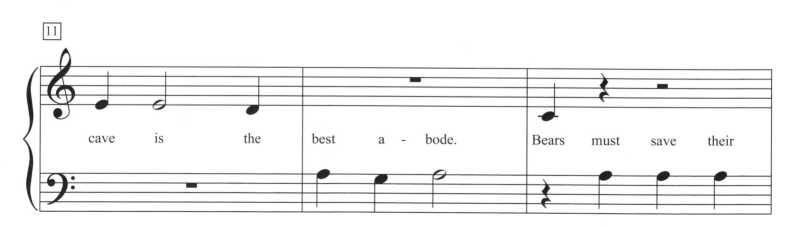

cave is the best a - bode. Bears must save their

en - er - gy. Rest all win - ter, then they'll be

f

read - y for spring to come! Hun - gry for

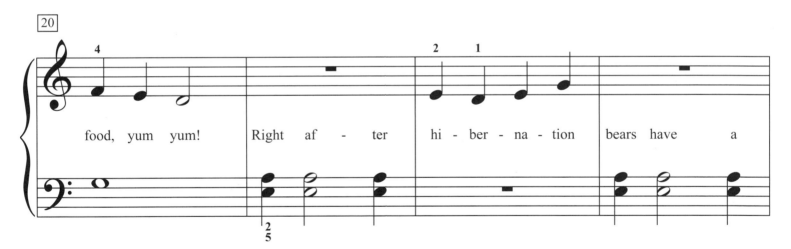

food, yum yum! Right af - ter hi - ber - na - tion bears have a

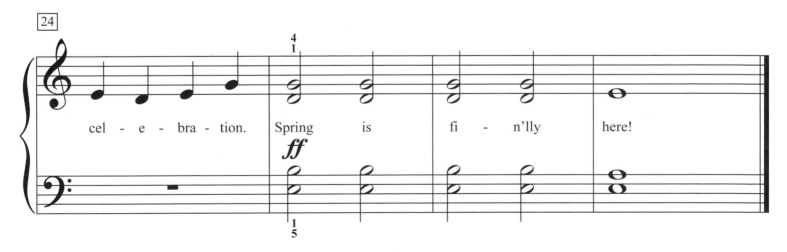

cel - e - bra - tion. Spring is fi - n'lly here!

ff

Tired Turtle

Jennifer Linn

Slow and steady ($\boldsymbol{\mathsf{d.}}$ = 44)

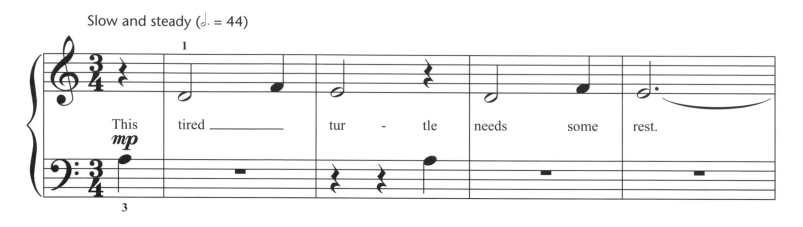

This tired _____ tur - tle needs some rest.

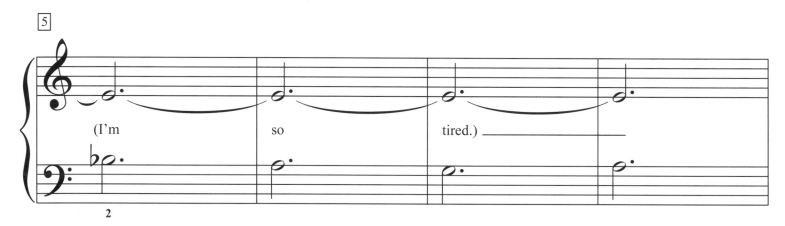

(I'm so tired.) _____

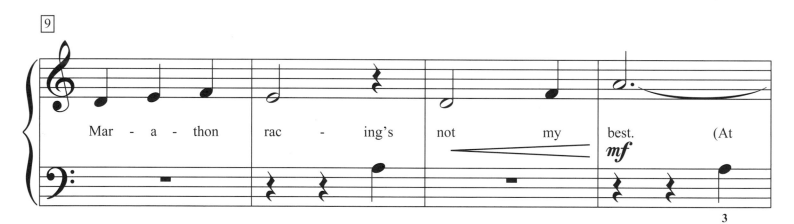

Mar - a - thon rac - ing's not my best. (At

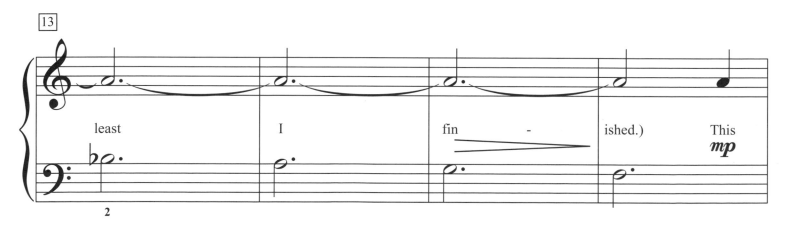

least I fin - ished.) This

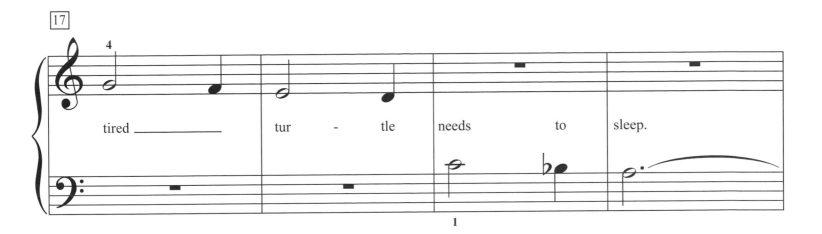

tired _____ tur - tle needs to sleep.

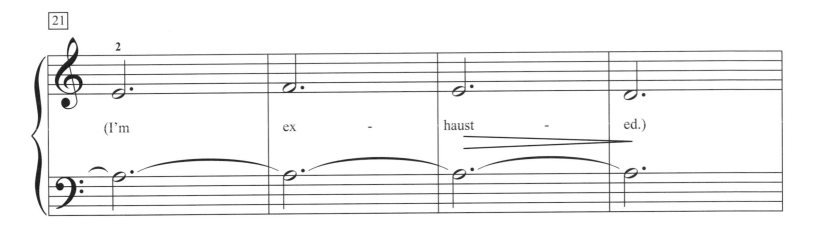

(I'm ex - haust - ed.)

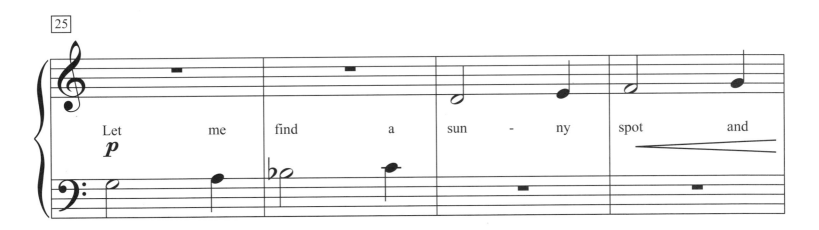

Let me find a sun - ny spot and
p

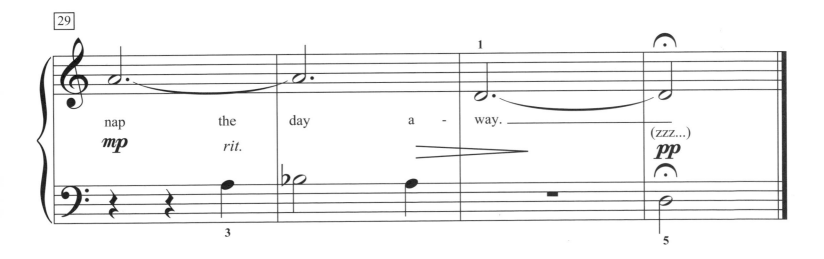

nap the day a - way. _____ (zzz...)
mp *rit.* **pp**

Understanding Whale

Jennifer Linn

Go with the flow (♩ = 132)

optional: depress damper pedal to the end

(Note to teacher: may be taught by rote)

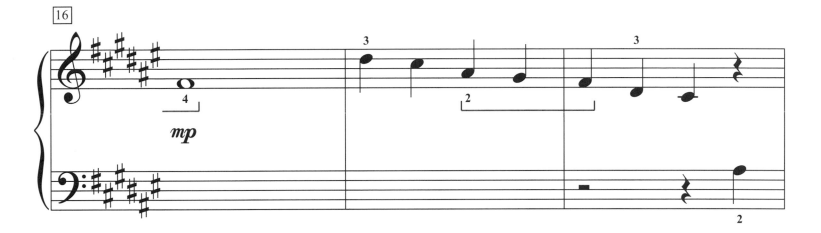

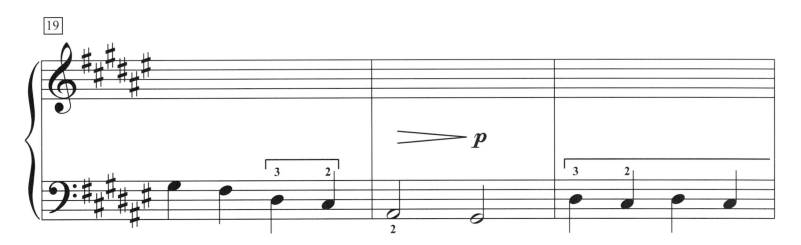

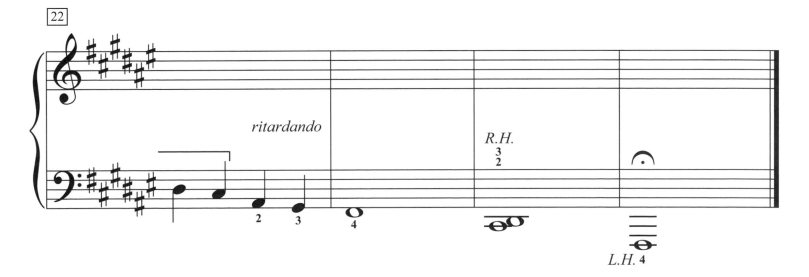

9

One Worried Owl

Jennifer Linn

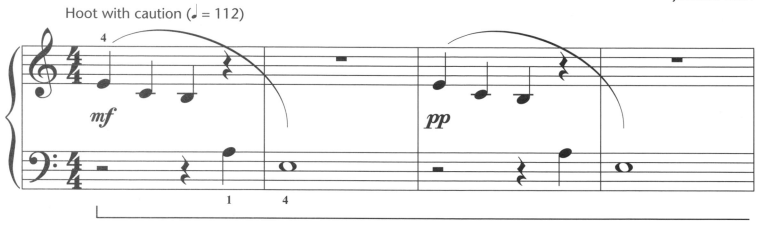

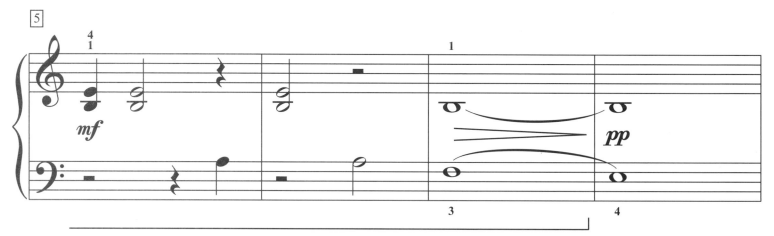

Elementary

Cheerful Chihuahua

Jennifer Linn

Cheerfully (♩ = 144)

I am the cheer - ful chi - hua - hua!

Be op - ti - mis - tic like me!

You can be sad if you wan - na. But

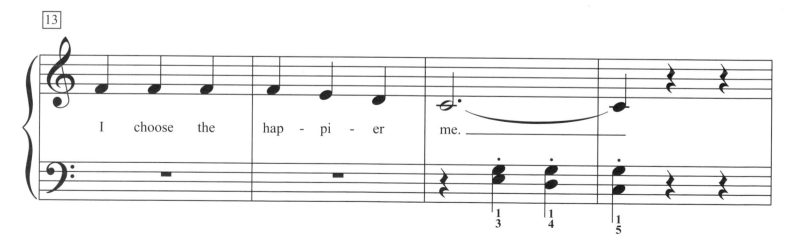

I choose the hap - pi - er me.

Look! Look! Look on the bright side!

Up! Up! Up to the up - side!

Keep! Keep! Keep a

pos - i - tive at - ti - tude.

A Giraffe Can Laugh

Jennifer Linn

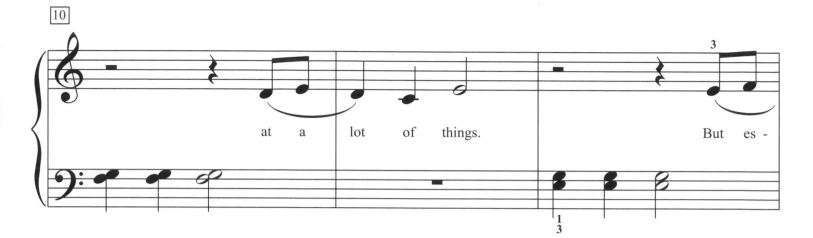

at a   lot   of   things.   But   es -

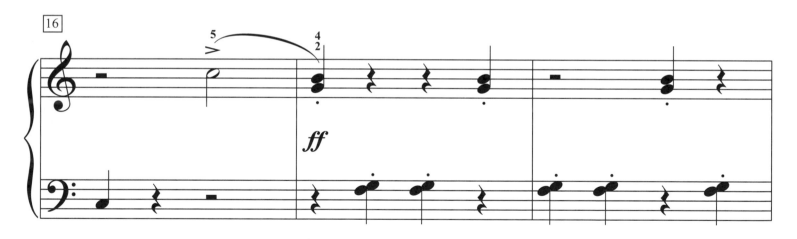

pe - cial - ly   he   can   laugh   at   him - self!

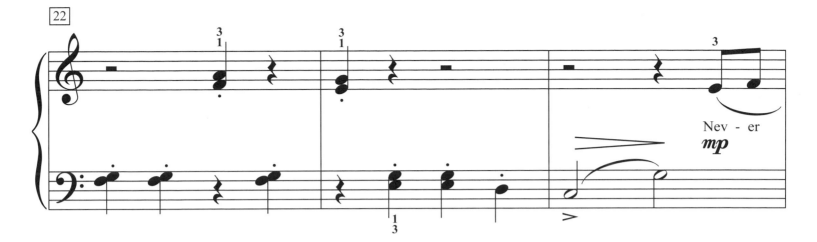

thought of that?　　　　　　　A gi - raffe can laugh!

(Spoken:) A gi - raffe can　laugh and so can　you!

Cry of the Wolf

Jennifer Linn

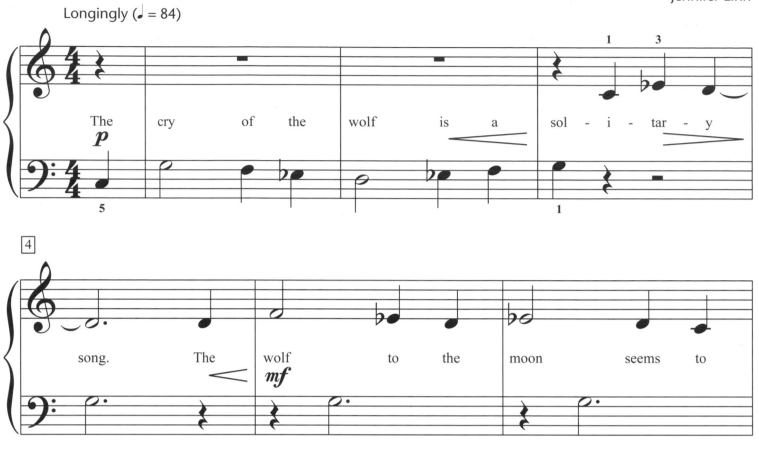

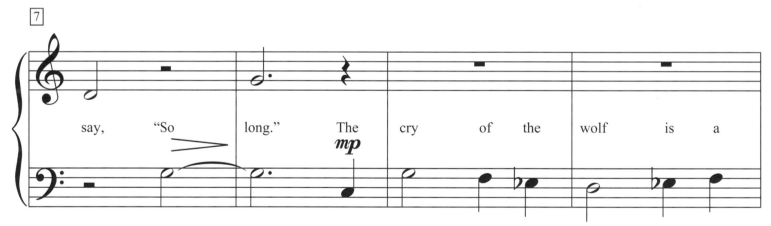

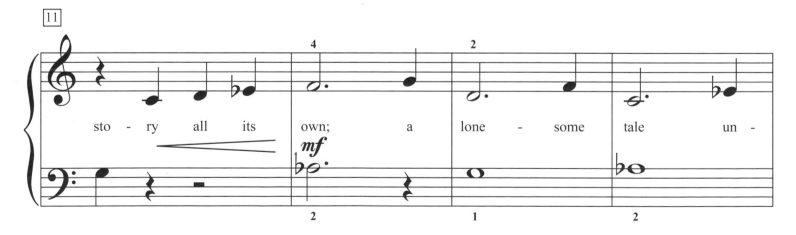

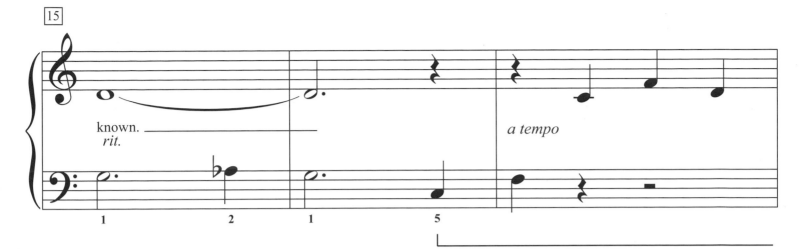

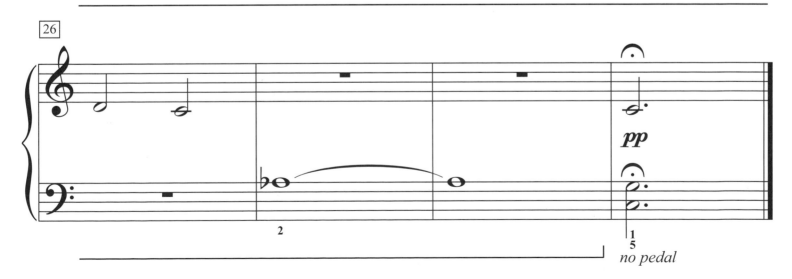

Mad Mad Cat

Jennifer Linn

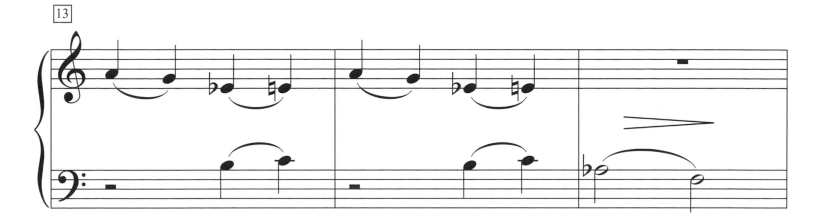

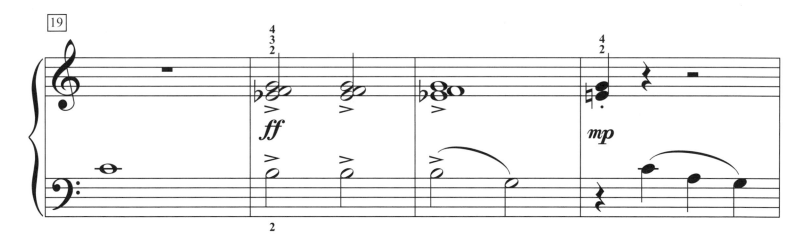

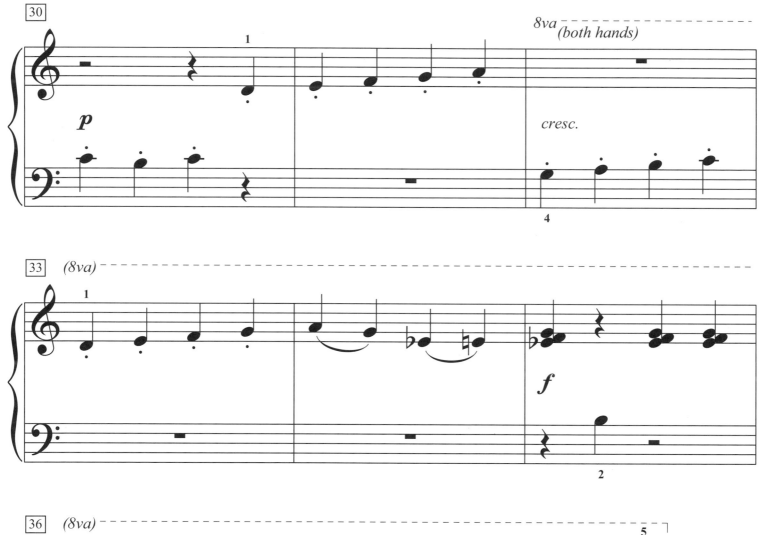

Hal Leonard Student Piano Library

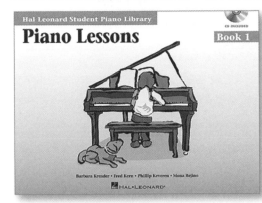

The Hal Leonard Student Piano Library has great music and solid pedagogy delivered in a truly creative and comprehensive method. It's that simple. A creative approach to learning using solid pedagogy and the best music produces skilled musicians! Great music means motivated students, inspired teachers and delighted parents. It's a method that encourages practice, progress, confidence, and best of all – success.

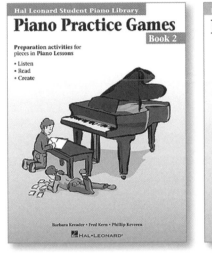  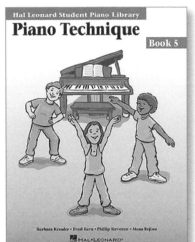

PIANO LESSONS BOOK 1
00296177 Book/Enhanced CD Pack $8.99
00296001 Book Only.....................................$6.99

PIANO PRACTICE GAMES BOOK 1
00296002 ....$6.99

PIANO SOLOS BOOK 1
00296568 Book/Enhanced CD Pack $8.99
00296003 Book Only.....................................$6.99

PIANO THEORY WORKBOOK BOOK 1
00296023 ....$6.99

PIANO TECHNIQUE BOOK 1
00296563 Book/Enhanced CD Pack $8.99
00296105 Book Only.....................................$6.99

NOTESPELLER FOR PIANO BOOK 1
00296088 ....$6.99

TEACHER'S GUIDE BOOK 1
00296048 ....$7.99

PIANO LESSONS BOOK 2
00296178 Book/Enhanced CD Pack $8.99
00296006 Book Only.....................................$6.99

PIANO PRACTICE GAMES BOOK 2
00296007 ....$6.99

PIANO SOLOS BOOK 2
00296569 Book/Enhanced CD Pack $8.99
00296008 Book Only.....................................$6.99

PIANO THEORY WORKBOOK BOOK 2
00296024 ....$6.99

PIANO TECHNIQUE BOOK 2
00296564 Book/Enhanced CD Pack $8.99
00296106 Book Only.....................................$6.99

NOTESPELLER FOR PIANO BOOK 2
00296089 ....$6.99

TEACHER'S GUIDE BOOK 2
00296362 ....$6.95

PIANO LESSONS BOOK 3
00296179 Book/Enhanced CD Pack $8.99
00296011 Book Only.....................................$6.99

PIANO PRACTICE GAMES BOOK 3
00296012 ....$6.99

PIANO SOLOS BOOK 3
00296570 Book/Enhanced CD Pack $8.99
00296013 Book Only.....................................$6.99

PIANO THEORY WORKBOOK BOOK 3
00296025 ....$6.99

PIANO TECHNIQUE BOOK 3
00296565 Book/Enhanced CD Pack $8.99
00296114 Book Only.....................................$6.99

NOTESPELLER FOR PIANO BOOK 3
00296167 ....$6.99

PIANO LESSONS BOOK 4
00296180 Book/Enhanced CD Pack $8.99
00296026 Book Only.....................................$6.99

PIANO PRACTICE GAMES BOOK 4
00296027 ....$6.99

PIANO SOLOS BOOK 4
00296571 Book/Enhanced CD Pack $8.99
00296028 Book Only.....................................$6.99

PIANO THEORY WORKBOOK BOOK 4
00296038 ....$6.99

PIANO TECHNIQUE BOOK 4
00296566 Book/Enhanced CD Pack $8.99
00296115 Book Only.....................................$6.99

PIANO LESSONS BOOK 5
00296181 Book/Enhanced CD Pack $8.99
00296041 Book Only.....................................$6.99

PIANO SOLOS BOOK 5
00296572 Book/Enhanced CD Pack $8.99
00296043 Book Only.....................................$6.99

PIANO THEORY WORKBOOK BOOK 5
00296042 ....$6.99

PIANO TECHNIQUE BOOK 5
00296567 Book/Enhanced CD Pack $8.99
00296116 Book Only.....................................$6.99

ALL-IN-ONE PIANO LESSONS
00296761 Book A – Book/Enhanced CD Pack $10.99
00296776 Book B – Book/Enhanced CD Pack $10.99
00296851 Book C – Book/Enhanced CD Pack $10.99
00296852 Book D – Book/Enhanced CD Pack $10.99

7777 W. BLUEMOUND RD. P.O. BOX 13819 MILWAUKEE, WI 53213

www.halleonard.com

Prices, contents, and availability subject to change without notice.

0214

This series showcases great original piano music from our **Hal Leonard Student Piano Library** family of composers, including Bill Boyd, Phillip Keveren, Carol Klose, Jennifer Linn, Mona Rejino, Eugénie Rocherolle and more. Carefully graded for easy selection, each book contains gems that are certain to become tomorrow's classics!

BILL BOYD

JAZZ BITS (AND PIECES)
Early Intermediate Level
00290312 11 Solos..............$7.99

JAZZ DELIGHTS
Intermediate Level
00240435 11 Solos..............$7.99

JAZZ FEST
Intermediate Level
00240436 10 Solos..............$7.99

JAZZ PRELIMS
Early Elementary Level
00290032 12 Solos..............$6.99

JAZZ SKETCHES
Intermediate Level
00220001 8 Solos..............$7.99

JAZZ STARTERS
Elementary Level
00290425 10 Solos..............$6.99

JAZZ STARTERS II
Late Elementary Level
00290434 11 Solos..............$7.99

JAZZ STARTERS III
Late Elementary Level
00290465 12 Solos..............$7.99

THINK JAZZ!
Early Intermediate Level
00290417 Method Book..............$10.99

TONY CARAMIA

JAZZ MOODS
Intermediate Level
00296728 8 Solos..............$6.95

SUITE DREAMS
Intermediate Level
00296775 4 Solos..............$6.99

SONDRA CLARK

DAKOTA DAYS
Intermediate Level
00296521 5 Solos..............$6.95

FAVORITE CAROLS FOR TWO
Intermediate Level
00296530 5 Duets..............$7.99

FLORIDA FANTASY SUITE
Intermediate Level
00296766 3 Duets..............$7.95

ISLAND DELIGHTS
Intermediate Level
00296666 4 Solos..............$6.95

THREE ODD METERS
Intermediate Level
00296472 3 Duets..............$6.95

MATTHEW EDWARDS

CONCERTO FOR YOUNG PIANISTS
FOR 2 PIANOS, FOUR HANDS
Intermediate Level Book/CD
00296356 3 Movements $16.95

CONCERTO NO. 2 IN G MAJOR
FOR 2 PIANOS, 4 HANDS
Intermediate Level Book/CD
00296670 3 Movements..............$16.95

PHILLIP KEVEREN

MOUSE ON A MIRROR
Late Elementary Level
00296361 5 Solos..............$6.95

MUSICAL MOODS
Elementary/Late Elementary Level
00296714 7 Solos..............$5.95

SHIFTY-EYED BLUES
Late Elementary Level
00296374 5 Solos..............$6.99

TEX-MEX REX
Late Elementary Level
00296353 6 Solos..............$5.95

CAROL KLOSE

CORAL REEF SUITE
Late Elementary Level
00296354 7 Solos..............$6.99

DESERT SUITE
Intermediate Level
00296667 6 Solos..............$7.99

FANCIFUL WALTZES
Early Intermediate Level
00296473 5 Solos..............$7.95

GARDEN TREASURES
Late Intermediate Level
00296787 5 Solos..............$7.99

ROMANTIC EXPRESSIONS
Intermediate/Late Intermediate Level
00296923 5 Solos..............$8.99

WATERCOLOR MINIATURES
Early Intermediate Level
00296848 7 Solos..............$7.99

JENNIFER LINN

AMERICAN IMPRESSIONS
Intermediate Level
00296471 6 Solos..............$7.99

CHRISTMAS IMPRESSIONS
Intermediate Level
00296706 8 Solos..............$6.99

JUST PINK
Elementary Level
00296722 9 Solos..............$6.99

LES PETITES IMAGES
Late Elementary Level
00296664 7 Solos..............$7.99

LES PETITES IMPRESSIONS
Intermediate Level
00296355 6 Solos..............$7.99

REFLECTIONS
Late Intermediate Level
00296843 5 Solos..............$7.99

TALES OF MYSTERY
Intermediate Level
00296769 6 Solos..............$8.99

MONA REJINO

CIRCUS SUITE
Late Elementary Level
00296665 5 Solos..............$5.95

JUST FOR KIDS
Elementary Level
00296840 8 Solos..............$7.99

MERRY CHRISTMAS MEDLEYS
Intermediate Level
00296799 5 Solos..............$7.99

PORTRAITS IN STYLE
Early Intermediate Level
00296507 6 Solos..............$7.99

EUGÉNIE ROCHEROLLE

**ENCANTOS ESPAÑOLES
(SPANISH DELIGHTS)**
Intermediate Level
00125451 6 Solos..............$7.99

JAMBALAYA
FOR 2 PIANOS, 8 HANDS
Intermediate Level
00296654 Piano Ensemble..............$9.99

JAMBALAYA
FOR 2 PIANOS, 4 HANDS
Intermediate Level
00296725 Piano Duo (2 Pianos)..............$7.95

TOUR FOR TWO
Late Elementary Level
00296832 6 Duets..............$7.99

TREASURES
Late Elementary/Early Intermediate Level
00296924 7 Solos..............$8.99

CHRISTOS TSITSAROS

DANCES FROM AROUND THE WORLD
Early Intermediate Level
00296688 7 Solos..............$6.95

LYRIC BALLADS
Intermediate/Late Intermediate Level
00102404 6 Solos..............$8.99

POETIC MOMENTS
Intermediate Level
00296403 8 Solos..............$8.99

SONATINA HUMORESQUE
Late Intermediate Level
00296772 3 Movements $6.99

SONGS WITHOUT WORDS
Intermediate Level
00296506 9 Solos..............$7.95

THREE PRELUDES
Early Advanced Level
00130747 ....$8.99

THROUGHOUT THE YEAR
Late Elementary Level
00296723 12 Duets..............$6.95

ADDITIONAL COLLECTIONS

ALASKA SKETCHES
by Lynda Lybeck-Robinson
Early Intermediate Level
00119637 8 Solos..............$7.99

AMERICAN PORTRAITS
by Wendy Stevens
Intermediate Level
00296817 6 Solos..............$7.99

AN AWESOME ADVENTURE
by Lynda Lybeck-Robinson
Late Elementary Level
00137563..............$7.99

AT THE LAKE
by Elvina Pearce
Elementary/Late Elementary Level
00131642 10 Solos and Duets..............$7.99

COUNTY RAGTIME FESTIVAL
by Fred Kern
Intermediate Level
00296882 7 Rags..............$7.99

PLAY THE BLUES!
by Luann Carman (Method Book)
Early Intermediate Level
00296357 10 Solos..............$9.99

HAL•LEONARD® CORPORATION
7777 W. BLUEMOUND RD. P.O. BOX 13819 MILWAUKEE, WI 53213